Animal World

THE DUCK

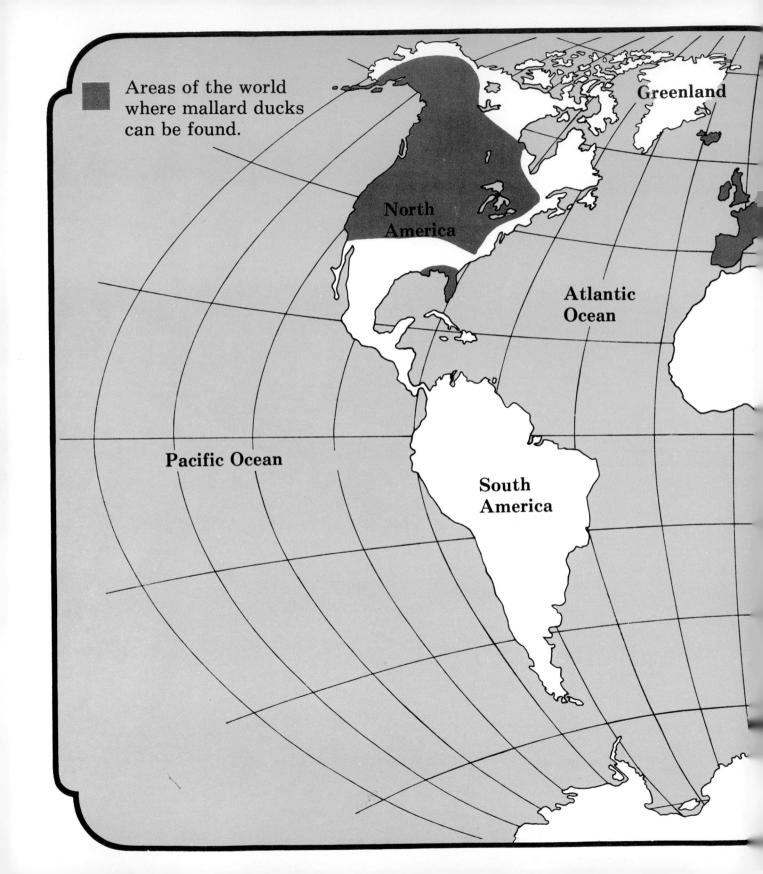

Areas of the world where mallard ducks can be found.

Greenland

North America

Atlantic Ocean

Pacific Ocean

South America

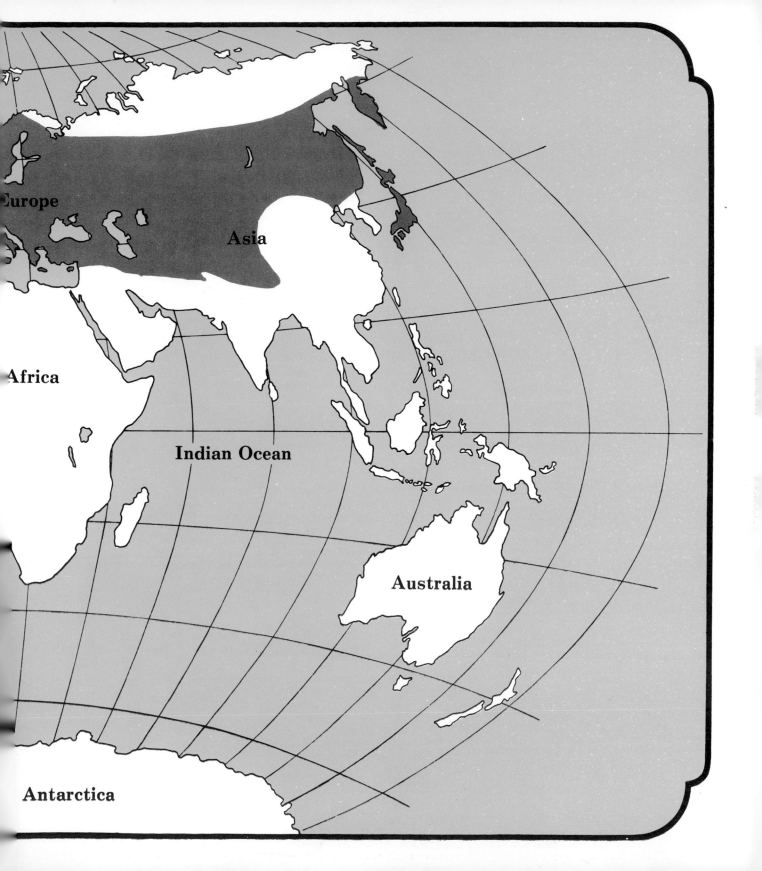

Europe

Asia

Africa

Indian Ocean

Australia

Antarctica

Published by The Rourke Enterprises, Inc., P.O. Box 711, Windermere, Florida 32786.
Copyright © 1983 by The Rourke Enterprises, Inc. All copyrights reserved. No part of this
book may be reproduced in any form without written permission from the publisher.
Printed in the United States of America.

Library of Congress Cataloging in Publication Data

Dalmais, Anne-Marie, 1954-
  The duck.

  (Animal world)
  Translation of: Le colvert.
  Reprint. Originally published: London : Macdonald
Educational, 1979.
  Summary: Describes the natural environment,
physical characteristics, and behavior of wild ducks,
emphasizing the life of the mallard.
  1. Mallard — Juvenile literature.   [1. Mallard.
2. Ducks]   I. Barrett, Peter, 1935-   ill.   II. Title.
III. Series.
QL696.A52D3413   1979   598.4'1   83-9783
ISBN 0-86592-862-2

Animal World

THE DUCK

illustrated by
Peter Barrett

ROURKE ENTERPRISES, INC.
Windermere, FL 32786

Ducks on a pond

It is springtime. The water of a big pond in the country is sparkling in the sunshine. Growing around the edge are reeds and rushes.

A pair of wild ducks have landed on the water. They are called mallards. The pond will be their new home.

They have not come to the pond by chance. It is close to where the female duck was born. They have flown a long way looking for it. This journey is called the ducks' spring migration.

Male and female

It is easy to tell which is the male duck, or drake. He has brilliant green feathers on his head and neck. There are other bright colors in his plumage, too. On each wing there is a blue area called a speculum.

The female's plumage is not as colorful. It is a muddy brown. When she is sitting on the nest they have made, it is difficult to see her because the surrounding reeds are almost the same color as her feathers.

Nine ducklings

When the nest was ready, the female laid nine pale green eggs in it. She covered them with bits of grass to hide them. Then she sat on the nest for 28 days and hatched them.

Each time she left the nest to look for food, she pulled soft downy feathers from her plumage and put them on top of the eggs.

Yesterday, nine small ducklings broke out of their shells and began to cheep loudly. Here they are with their mother. They are yellow and dark brown. For the first few hours they stayed close to the nest, getting warm and building up their strength. Then they set out eagerly on their first walk.

Today their mother is teaching them to swim. See how they follow her in a line.

Ducklings
have a huge appetite

The ducklings hardly ever stop eating. They are never satisfied. They plunge their heads into the water, paddle about and poke their beaks into the mud. They bring out small fish, plants, tadpoles and sometimes frogs. They also like to glide over the surface of the pond gobbling up flying insects such as dragonflies and mosquitoes as they go.

Today, the banks of the pond are covered with slugs and snails because it has been raining. What a feast for the ducklings.

Friends and enemies

The mallards do not have the pond to themselves. Some of the creatures which share it are shown in this picture. There is the black moorhen that eats water lilies, the shoveller duck with its big flat beak, the crested grebe with its babies on its back and a tall heron standing all alone. There is also the furry water vole.

These are its friends, but it has enemies too.

The ducklings have only one way of escaping. They hide under water, with just their beaks poking out.

Growing up

A few weeks have passed. Now it is summer and the days are getting longer. It is warmer, too, and yellow iris flowers are growing by the pond.

The ducklings are much bigger and their yellow down is now covered with beautiful brown and gray feathers like their mother's. Once they have grown these feathers, the ducklings look much more like their parents.

They still cannot fly, but they never get tired of swimming. They dart about all over the big oval pond. They especially like those parts where the watercress and water lilies grow. Another favorite is the patch of reeds around the edge.

Sometimes their father, the great mallard drake, comes for a short visit. Here you can see him landing on the water with his legs stretched out in front of him. He is now in his duller summer plumage. His feathers are brown and gray like those of the female duck.

The wonder of flying

In the fine, warm weather of summer, the ducklings are ready to fly. One by one, they open their wings, stretch them, flap them and then take off smoothly. Leaving the pond behind them, they fly away together on a new adventure.

Soon they are gliding over the surrounding countryside with its towns, farms and lush green fields and trees. It is all very strange to them. They have never seen such things as houses and farm animals before. At the end of their outing they return to the pond.

Molting

It is the end of the summer and the colors of the leaves are beginning to change. It is also molting time for the ducks. Whenever they shake their wings, feathers drop out. During this time they do not feel strong enough to fly, so they stay quietly among the reeds.

After several days the new feathers begin to grow. Four of the young ducks have the same brilliant plumage as their father, the drake. The other five have the light brown coloring of their mother.

They are all very proud of their new feathers and display themselves on the shore of the pond.

The ducks migrate

Now that they are fully grown, the ducks are able to fly off on their first migration. This is the long journey south, away from the winter cold to lands where the sun shines.

Before they leave, other ducks come and join them at their pond. There is a great noise of quacking and the fluttering of wings. Then, suddenly, they all take off. They fly in two lines in the shape of a huge arrowhead. They move swiftly across the sky.

SOME INTERESTING FACTS ABOUT DUCKS

Species:

Most ducks are aquatic birds, which simply means that they spend most of their lives in the water. Ducks are closely related to geese and swans. However, ducks are smaller.

There are twenty-two species of sea ducks. They live on the cold, northern coasts by the oceans. Examples are the eider, the scoter and the goldeneye. Sea ducks are stout and generally brightly colored. They are clumsy on land, but they are beautiful swimmers and excellent divers. The eider duck of the far north can dive to a depth of one hundred and eighty feet. Merganser ducks have even been known to chase fish underwater. Sea ducks eat shellfish, sea urchins, squid and fish.

There are thirteen species of perching ducks. This type of duck makes its nest in a hole in a tree. Some nests are as high as sixty feet above ground. The most colorful duck in North America belongs to this species. It is the Carolina wood duck. As in many cases, the male is brightly colored. The female is rather plain. The Mandarin duck of Asia is another handsome perching duck.

There are fourteen species of fresh water ducks. These are generally medium-sized ducks that live in ponds or in the grasses by a river. The most sought after "sporting" duck, the canvasback, belongs to this species. You may have seen ringnecks and redheads floating on lakes. When they spot some food they dive underwater to get it.

The most common duck in the United States is the mallard. It is a fresh water duck. The mallard is the ancestor of all our domestic ducks, except the Muscovy. Mallards are swift fliers. They can reach speeds of sixty miles per hour. However, they are slow swimmers. Because mallards are considered good game birds, they must always be on the alert for hunters.

Muscovy ducks and turkeys are the only domestic birds which originated in the New World.

Description:

Ducks spend most of their lives in water. Their bodies are designed for this type of life.

A duck's body is surrounded by a layer of fat. This fat gives the duck bouyancy in water. It also provides warmth for northern ducks who live in the icy ocean.

If you look at the leg of a bird you can tell how far it will wade out to get food. Ducks have short, stumpy legs. They are more likely to dive than wade. The foot is paddle shaped and the toes are webbed. This propels it through water. Some fresh water ducks can spring from the water to the air in an instant because their leg muscles are so strong. This is a great help in escaping enemies. Diving ducks must run on the surface of the water to become airborne.

Study a duck's bill and you can figure out how it gets its food. Some ducks have bills that are flat and have holes around them. This type of duck takes in gulps of food and water. The bill holds the food and the water escapes through the holes. Some ducks have long, pointed bills. These are good for probing the muddy bottom of a pond.

The duck is smaller in size than his cousins, the swans and geese. The average duck measures between seventeen and twenty-one inches long. It weighs between one and a half and three pounds.

Most ducks live twenty years.

Conservation:

Ducks have no natural protection against enemies. They have no teeth and claws, like a dog. They have no venom, like a snake. They do not have a horrible smell, like a skunk. They are not as swift as a cat. If attacked, the only thing that a duck can do is hide underwater.

To protect themselves from man some ducks will hunt for food at night and sleep during the day.

In general, ducks do not seem to be in danger of extinction. An exception to this is the European eider duck. The eider's down is very valuable because it is used to make quilts. For this reason men hunted it almost to extinction on three separate occasions. Scandanavia and Iceland have now passed laws protecting the eider.

The last species to actually become extinct was the Labrador duck. The last one seen was spotted on Long Island, New York in 1875.